Dead Men Reading Post Cards
Poems

Some of these poems appeared in slightly different forms in

Creativity Webzine
Empty Window
Front Window
Inbetweenhangovers
Magnum Opus Anthology
Nixes Mate
Shelia na-gig

Thank you to the editors of those publications

Cover art by Gene McCormick
Copyright© 2022 Alan Catlin
ISBN: 978-81-8253-950-1
Cyberwit.net

Contents

This project is the result of over a decade of composition. Every year since 1991 my wife and I traveled from Upstate N.Y. to Block Island, off the coast of Rhode Island, to stay with her aunt who retired to the Island. After she moved back on to the mainland, we bought a time share on a hill overlooking the aunt's house. My friend and fellow poet Dave Church lived in providence, R.I., and we would pass the city on our trip to and from the ferry from the point at the base of the state. Every year I would write a post card to Dave from the same spot overlooking the harbor and mail it from the post office nearby. Every year I threatened to stop by for a visit and every year we did not do so usually because of time (or weather) constraints. Then Dave died unexpectedly and I felt the keen loss of a connection I could have made but didn't. Every year after his death I continued to write a post card to Dave even though now I would never mail them. (except for 2020 when we didn't go to Block Island or anywhere else for that matter). Some of those are included in the connection.

The bulk of these cards were sent to poet, artist, photographer and mail art guru David Thompson who sends out bulk mailings of cards to select list of friends, acquaintances, poets and fellow artists. As many of them were art related, I decided why should he have all the fun and decided to respond in kind to as many of his cards as I could. The responses became a kind of ekphrastic challenge and the project lasted over a year. The ones I responded to here refer to a particular picture on his cards referenced in the titles. Other, occasional cards, were to people I sometimes send poems to from Block Island or random cards that turned up during the project. The writing of these began before and lasted into the pandemic year(s) but could have been any time in recent history, hence the non-specified yearly dates. Also, some of these were taken out of order of their composition so specific dates seemed to me potentially, and unnecessarily, confusing.

To Dave Church taxi driver, poet of the people, friend, who died behind the wheel

and to the people these were inspired by or "written" to including, among others:

David Thompson
TK Splake
Gene McCormick
Stephanie Hiteshew
Steve Dalachinsky
Randy Meeks

In Memoriam
Richard T Scally
John Conway
Richard Costa
Steve Dalachinsky

Hey Churchman,

      What's wrong with me?
Writing poems to a dead guy.
Good question there is no good
answer to. I suppose one way to
look at this is a literal way: there
is no time like the present? What
does that even mean: no time like
the present? Does it mean we've
run out of time? Or the present is
out of time or....
      What I do know is no one
Writes to you like this once I'm gone.
I'll keep us both alive as long as
I can. peace brother

Post Card to Church in Providence
on a Monday Night

It's raining and cold this April night
after a ridiculously warm Winter.
This is one of those nights that makes
you think of that impossible-to-forget-
but-not-in-a-good-way, Harry Chapin song
you must have hated. After a while, driving
hack, it isn't about making your night with
a tip but making it through the night.
What might seem like cheap sentiment
has a lot of truth in it when you are behind
the wheel and you never know what you are
picking up next. Maybe the next one is the
ride that will punch your ticket. It happens.
We both know the feeling. Working
Monday nights in the bar were like that for
me. After I wrote "A New Year's Eve
Bash" about the bartender who got stomped
to death in Albany. On a Monday. You were
one of the few who never bothered to ask if
that really happened. Why would you make
something like that up?
Slow nights I locked up early, double
checked the place was secure, and did some
serious drinking. No public transport
running then. Not even the milk train. I'd
just have to wait it out alone. After all there
was plenty of hooch and a jukebox, if I
needed something that was louder than the
silence of 4 A.M. Even now, years after
you're gone, I think it is still about making

it through the night. You're way beyond that
now. I have so much catching up to do.

Post Card to Splake October 20:
Noir Night on a Lost Highway

Dear TK,
        Getting some of your fine UP
weather. Last of the changed leaves
getting ripped from the trees. At least,
the sideways rain of last Sunday has held
off. Who needs that on a ferry ride to
the mainland? Much too Edmund
Fitzgerald for me.
        A murder of crows is gathering
in the trees in the hollow just below the
airport. Makes me wonder what's dead
down there. Hopefully, nothing human.
No sunset tonight.

Nov. 21, 20-- Post Card to
Thompson: Camus

Every time I think of Camus
now, I think of reading *The Fall*
in the gallery between juror
interviews at one of the murder
trials I got a jury summons for.
This was a mistaken identity/
turf killing, a senseless one,
as they so often are, but one
with a motive: "Don't tread on my
turf, bro." The dead guy was a
baller point guard for a while, until
the drugs took over his life. Had the
same name as one of my favorite
NBA players who should have been
rookie of the year but they gave
it to Patrick Ewing instead,
a guy who missed almost half a
season. Gave it to him because he
was, well, Patrick Ewing and he
was destined to have a Hall of
Fame career. Fuck Xavier
McDaniel. Our Xavier McDaniel III
is bound for nowhere now. Like
Camus, dead in the front seat of a
car on a hot summer day.

Post Card to McCormick: October 20--

Dear Gene,

They say it gets cold in the desert
at night but not like here; sideways rain
and a bit of snow in October. Like some-
thing from Hokusai: One Hundred Views
of Mt Fuji, peasants bent beneath an
elemental force, earthly burdens, trudging
uphill. From here, sometimes, you can see
Long Island. If you wanted to. I don't share
Gatsby's nostalgia for the Island. I'd much
rather see Mt. Fuji, even an unflattering
view.
Increasing winds bringing storm
clouds. the Sound will be all riptides and
white caps; the North Point lighthouse a
blur in the wild, wind-driven rain.

Post Card to Stephanie October 20--

It's clear here and cool, totally
unlike the storms you've been having.
From where I'm sitting overlooking
the Old Harbor, I can see the mainland.
Nearby, they are replacing the old dock
and building anew. The crane they are
using to remove the old pylons and ties
sways back and forth like a great steel
metronome.

We walked the beach today by
the North Point Lighthouse. Since we'd
last been, new dunes have been created
as if a large part of the beach had been
swept away by a terrible rip tide creating
a new Grand Canyon of sand. Soon this
too will be washed away.

Post Card to Thompson, Nov. 30, 20--:
Charlotte Rampling

On a beach, she was an image of
stardust memoires dancing to the
music of time, mock Bergman style.
Was "half-crazy and you touched her
perfect body with your mind", as L. Cohen
said about another woman named Suzanne.
The actress wore a Nazi cap in a night
porter's lair, was a sex slave whose lust
transcended time. Was a kind of Cindy
Sherman still on a cutting room floor,
a European noir fantasy woman in
a black and white flick that was never
made, was a kind of Lolita all grown up
and streetwalking in a dream. Back alleys
became her. Nuns gave her rosary beads
every time she passed, her sly suggestion
of something like a smile reveals all.

Hey Churchman,

I thought about you last time I
was downtown Albany for a reading.
I left the bar where the reading was
and called for a ride uptown to another
bar. Cabbie asked me, "Where to?"
And I said, "WT's." "How come you
want to go there, it's like a scum bar?"
"I work there." The ride was nice and
quiet after that. So, what I wanted to
know was, isn't it bad for tips to criticize
a fare's destination? Not that I wasn't
rudeness personified when I tended bar.
People used to ask me, "How do you
make any money?" And I used to say,
"Volume." Sleep with the angels my friend.

Post Card to Dalachinsky Dec.1, 20--
      Channeling Dave Church

All those times Dave drove hookers
home after work. Some of them almost
beautiful, he said, a little high or worse,
all of them flirty angling for a free ride
or something else. Dave said it wasn't good
business to take fares in trade but
sometimes they paid and took you inside
anyway. Or in the back seat. They may have
been as short of ready as they said, may not
have been either, but all of them were
convincing.   A good story meant a lot to
him. He said they were preferable to the
college kids, drunk on their ass, obnoxious,
especially when he demanded the fare up
front. More than one said, "Fuck off long
hair," and hailed another hack. More than
once he dared them to take him on. None of
them did. The ones sober enough to speak,
who looked almost human, he gave a quiz,
"If you can spell Schenectady, I'll give you
a free ride." A couple could, and he did.
One even shook your hand after and said,
"It was a pleasure riding with you."
Sometimes it really is the little things in life
that count. I'm keeping track of them for
Dave now that he can't. I hope it's warmer
where you are than it is here.

Post Card to Thompson December 4, 20--:
Brando in *The Wild One*

Whenever I think of Brando
now, I see Kurtz in his cave
cooling himself with handfuls
of water, only partially visible
in shadow light, alternately reciting
Eliot and articulating some mad,
nihilistic vision that sent him deep
into the jungle to assemble a rogue
army of Montagnard's, mercenaries,
soldiers of misfortune.... Critics said
his performance was opaque,
bloated like his body, incoherent....
I suspect they envisioned John Wayne
in fresh, pressed fatigues even after days
in the Green. Real heroes don't sweat.
Or maybe they wanted Col. Hawksworth,
a soldier for all seasons, battle tested,
brave and ready to engage again.
"All those tiny little arms." Kurtz
says, about the severed, mutilated,
inoculated by the enemy body parts.
"The horror, the horror."

Post Card to Splake Dec. 05, 20--:
Gable and Monroe, *The Misfits*

Maybe *The Misfits* should have
called *Last Tango in Las Vegas*.
Three main stars dead, unwittingly
playing roles in a last picture
show. Thelma R. hung around and
Eli W. lived forever, comparatively,
thriving in roles like the ugly guy
Tuco, in the last of Eastwood, Man
with No Name trilogy. No wonder
he didn't get Marilyn in *Misfits*
or the blonde in *Baby Doll* though
he sure made a great slime ball.
And poor Monty. His soulful eyes,
face turned away from the camera
to better conceal facial wounds suffered
in drunken car crash as he calls from a glass
phone booth. Calls home to assure his
mom everything was going to be okay.
As if it could ever be okay again.
In that movie or outside of it.
Some say James Dean was the tragic one.
How does he compare, really?
So young, untested, effete, effeminate,
almost; his best career move dying
young to insure immortality, screen
stardom for all time despite a slim
body of work. What did he accomplish,
really? Played chicken with Death and lost.

Post Card to Thompson Dec. 20--:
Battered Portable Typewriter

Looking at the old portable typer
I half expect pages to emerge,
unbidden, from a *Naked Lunch*,
as automatic writing, a chapter from
a kind of *Yage Letter*s novel, each
letter a different vision from a
hallucinating whole. Late at night,
the keys move themselves, making
impressions on onion skin paper,
each word hammered so hard,
the paper begins to bleed. In the morning,
exterminators spray for bugs but
vermin survive. You can hear them,
the rats, scuttling between floors,
tails poking tiny holes through the walls,
their red eyes peering in, all the better
to see you.

Post Card to Thompson Dec, 11, 20—
Dylan Thomas *Portrait of the Artist as
a Young Dog*

No one reads Brinnin's poetry anymore
and with good reason. But they do read
his memoir of arranging and accompanying
Dylan Thomas's infamous reading tours.
By inference, it was like shepherding one
of Satan's minions on a wild ride through
hell with all the drunken and sex fueled
escapades imaginable. If there was a
pub, Dylan would find it, even broke,
he would be backed up on the bar from
today until next week with free drunks.
He had a natural gift for finding bar flies
who felt obligated to buy him booze
and not feel cheated after, to feel honored,
even, to have done so. If there was an
available woman, preferably a rich and
generous one, he would meet her.
There had never been anyone like this.
Hasn't been since, on the poetry circuit,
in a time when people actually flocked
to hear poets read. It was the 50's and
rock stars hadn't been invented yet.
Hell, even Elvis, notorious as he was,
had yet to accede to the throne
as The King of Rock 'n Roll. In fact,
they were drafting him and shipping him
off to Germany where they could keep
an eye on him. That old tried and true
cultural threat reducer: neuter and

commercialize. Have you seen that Benz
commercial? "Oh Lord, won't you buy me
a Mercedes Benz..."If Janis wasn't dead,
that would have killed her. And Dylan,
what a miracle behind the microphone,
one minute he would be stumbling drunk,
the next, on the stage with his poems,
a sound check and then that mellifluous
baritone, "Rage, rage, rage, against the
dying of the light...."

Post Card to Thompson Dec. 13, 20--:
T. Monk

I wrote a poem once called "Self-
Portrait of the Artist with Thelonious
Monk." Everyone who read it, quite
understandably, thought it was about
the jazz pianist. In fact, the inspiration
came from a book jacket/ author portrait,
of one of America's greatest, prolific,
virtually unknown, brilliant writers,
Percival Everett, with one of his mules
who he named Thelonious Monk.
Everett used to raise mules, I don't know
if he still does, but it is clear, from that
snap, he dug that mule. Maybe as much as
the man's music. You'd have to ask him.
Everett that is. He probably would
appreciate the sleight of hand trick with the
title, given how he is a master of narrative
sleights himself. Especially in his novel,
Assumption, which begins with a cop
investigating a murder, with the typical
detective point of view.
Everett misleads you to think he is a good,
hard working, dedicated cop, an assumption
you probably shouldn't make, as in, you
fucked up (to paraphrase Animal House)
you trusted the author. Turns out the cop
killed the babe and took the drugs. He was
a thorough going bastard. Totally unlike
what you were led to believe early on.

I wrote the poem prior to reading
Assumption. I feel as if Everett and I were
kindred souls on the subject of point of
view. After all, point of view really is
everything. I must confess, by the time I
finished *Assumption*, I was saying
damn you Percival Everett. You
cheated. But did he, really?

Post Card to Church Oct. 20--

Hey Churchman,

      Still think of you every time we
come here. Rhode Island was your state,
Man, Providence, your home.
      I'm sitting on a bench overlooking
the Old Harbor, as usual, when I write.
The ferry has been and gone. No one much
comes here this far off-season, anyway.
Only fishermen, painters and old poets,
like us, and their wives.
      Warm, clear blue, cloudless sky.
A great day to be alive. I wish you were
still with us. I really wish you were here.

Postcards in Pieces to Thompson Dec. 24

That photo on the card could have
been my family. If my father wore a
cap and looked vaguely like Truffaut.
And if my parents hadn't divorced
well before this picture would have
been taken. And if my mother was blonde,
which she wasn't, and hadn't been locked
away for two years in a nuthouse,
When I had grown to the age to be
somewhat like that smiling boy.
Who was so like me: the haircut,
the round face, the eager- looking-for
approval/attention look.
An only child. I was so insular, even then.
It is difficult to imagine ever being happy.

Christmas Post Card 20--

What I could imagine is being in a drive-in
movie in the rain. Mother did things like
that. We could not have seen *400 Blows,*
as it hadn't been made yet. She would have
liked Truffaut movies like *Don't Shoot the
Piano Player.* She would have thought it
was about her. Like the *Phantom Woman*
which actually Was about her.

Mother was the kind of person who looked
the wrong way for traffic before signaling
all clear and stepping off the curb. Who
taught her child how to drown by placing
him in the deep end of a pool and
instructing him to swim.

Kids were born knowing how to do these
things. She just assumed all was well,
because in her world, it was. It was a fairy
world like a Charles Kingsley novel she
based her thinking on.

So, she read fashion magazines, while her
child sank in the clear chlorine drowning
pool. Never once looking to see how the
lesson was going. That was her way as well.

A Ghost Card to Dave Church in the After
Life

Hey Churchman,

Been a long time, bro. I know but
where you are now, time has no meaning.
It means everything to me now.
Not that it matters, we're all on
the brink of annihilation anyway. I know
we decided never to talk politics since we
disagreed about everything. Sometimes
you can't help it. We're this close to a Big
War, based on the whims and caprices of an
ignorant, narcissist child. And that's our
guy. The other guy is all of that plus crazy.
I'm not sure about our guy in the crazy
department.
Our war wasn't much better. Not
that either of us actually went. At least, the
college kids today don't have to live in
mortal fear of being drafted into the
Services and then be shipped off to a war no
one understood.
You told me most of your late night
business in the cab was college kids totally
drunk on their asses. You told them if they
even thought about puking in your cab it
would be the last thing they ever did. And
most of them believed you. You might not
have been ripped like Hulk Hogan but you
could pass for him otherwise.
I consider my so-called career in

the bar biz was penance for what I was like
when I was in college. I told that to Sharkey
once and he said, "Thirty-four years is one
hell of long penance." I guess I had a lot
to atone for. I still do. Sleep with the angels.

Post Card to Thompson Jan. 5, 20--:
Kitchen Confidential Revisited

They all had names like:
Cutter and Bone, Animal Mother
and Mad Dog. Wore head bands,
neck bands, wrist bands, to absorb
the sweat.
The really cool ones, the super
stars, wore samurai head wraps like
Christopher Walken in *Deer Hunter*
when he was doing his Russian Roulette
thing.
They were never women in the
kitchen, though they liked to fuck them.
Even the waitresses. Especially the
waitresses, who otherwise, were of no use at
all.
All the cooks agreed there was a
song about their lives called, *I Walk the Line*
and it was sung by a man in black.
They laughed when they said it but
no one thought it was a joke. They were all
crazy. Every single one of them. Maybe it
was the heat. Maybe they were born that
way. Maybe it came with the job.
If you worked in a restaurant, you
just had to go with it.
After all, they all had knives they
knew how to use.

Post Card to Thompson January 18, 20--

      Nightly, I dream of Sissy Spacek.
The young Sissy. And she is smiling,
standing among high weeds in a field,
wearing a cheap, store-bought print
dress she might have worn, dreaming
of meeting someone like Martin
Sheen, who would come and take her
away from all of this.
      When I reach out to touch her,
the original, pleasing image, is fouled
by gushing blood like some kind of
Carrie nightmare. Her face dissolves
like melting wax and white out is applied,
feature by feature.
      And then I am in another field.
An *Elvira Madigan* field, before the Nazis
came, and starvation became a way of
life, and there was nothing romantic
about it.
      Elvira, her lover, and I, can hear
Mozart in the distance, Concerto #21
for Piano and Orchestra.
      Musicians were often allowed
to live in the Camps, on slightly-more-
than-minimal rations, in death camps,
and would be forced to perform, often
at the most gruesome occasions and
celebrations imaginable.
      Nazis loved commemorative
events and music. They still do.

Post Card to RTS in the Afterlife
Jan. 29, 20-: *The Wild One*

Remember that iconic image
that was on every male college student's
wall, next to Bruce Lee, of Marlon Brando
on his motorcycle from the *Wild One*?
That was you, wasn't it?
Or how you saw yourself, though
you later acquired a Jap bike you dumped
more than once. At least, when I knew you,
back in the 70's, when we were primo
amigos. I wonder, were you ever able to
walk again without a limp?
You loved that poem I wrote about
you way back in the tavern days, "What I
Would Do If I Owned a Motorcycle". The
last lines were, "Bleed up the whole
Goddamned Road, yes, I would, if I owned
a motorcycle."
It was all about dying young, in a
spectacular fashion, not the way you went,
slowly, from a long illness, at 67.
That must have really put a dent in
your self-image. If you still had one, that is.
I wouldn't know, one way or the other, as
you, effectively, disappeared in the 80's and
no one much saw you afterwards. I'm not
sure if I want to hear the details. The
preliminary search I did on you, yielded so
many questions of a catastrophic nature, I
thought, maybe, it was better to remember
you when you were young, driving the top

down, bright green pleasure machine/death car, Triumph sports model, or the Jap bike, the wind in your face, bugs in your teeth, and a Belle Star helmet scuffed from road rash and who knew what else? It was fun for a while and then, well, it wasn't. Ride hard into the ozone, my friend. It's where you always wanted to be.

There were jazz bands in those
days. Dim lights, crowded tables, votive
candle four tops. Spot filters color
highlighting two hundred burning, long
ash cigarettes.

Dancers high heel kicking, tight ties
askew, suit jackets cast aside. Drinkers/
revelers red faced flush.

And we worked the lounges.
Listened to service bar snark: "Perfect Man-
the only perfect man you'll ever see has rye
whiskey in it, A Pink Lady Up for her, more
like a scarlet woman...."

Hours later, after the rush, chugging
shaker glasses of chilled scotch, blowing
demon weed, running red lights, heading
downtown for the last set of Amazing B
list show band playing The Post.

Watching as the drummer boy
warmed up for climactic set. Deep
breathing a plastic tube like *Blue Velvet*
Psycho, Frank. One last toke and he
launches into Gene Krupa riff. Blows us
back four rows, on stadium seating,
right up against heavy curtained windows,
in after-hours club, before the all-night card
games we were too stoned to play.

We were the Pros from Dover then.
Inseparable, crazy at work and play, up for
anything in either. No challenge too great,
no hangover too debilitating. We were in
some kind of Inagaddadavida haze, some

Steppenwolf fantasy, "...gonna fly so high,
never gonna die...."
		Laid out, I would never have
recognized you if your name wasn't printed
on a card: RTS Jr. And your brother was
shaking hands. Accepting condolences.
What happened to you, man? We were the
Pros from Dover....it wasn't just that we
grew old, slowed down. What was
it that made you, fundamentally, not you?
		I knew you well.
		I mean, I really knew you well.

Post Card to Sexton on Mercy Street

You must have been exhausted.
All that awful rowing toward God.
You dolled up for Death. Fixed
your make up. Your hair. Drank a shaker
full of chilled Gin. Popped some pills.
Plugged the car exhaust and turned
the engine over.
Something like that.
Reports vary but the end result
is always the same.
There are no reprieves, no second
chances once you've crossed the bar on
Mercy Street.

Post Card to Conway 20--

John,

        Maybe it was the shock of it all.
You dying so suddenly, nothing about it
seemed real. Even your memorial felt
somehow strange as if you'd stepped out
for a drink or a smoke or something and
a packed house was inside waiting for
you to come back so everyone could
yell: SURPRISE!
        Except the surprise is, there was
no coming back. You never smoked, that
I knew of, and I'd known you for 40 years.
I do know you hadn't had a drink for 25
years, maybe more.
        We talked about that a lot. Not
drinking, "After a while you get used to it."
Someone asked at the bar, I think it was
Ronnie the cop, whether you ever stopped
wanting it." You never stop wanting it."
        But you can't always get what you
want.
        It's so odd seeing people who look
like other people you know well walking
about as I did, you, the day after the
memorial. A double take doesn't quite
erase the image. The point is, I guess,
you're gone but I want to bring you back.
        Go in peace, my brother,

Post Card to Thompson March 14, 20--:
Black Sun

The black sun has just set behind
the snowcapped mountains. The Killing
Tree, in the foreground, is where they hang
men after no-trial judgments, creating cliché
scenes of holding-torches-men, mob
mayhem and noise, then the rope thrown
over a limb.

A man struggles against the violent
surge of the extraordinary delusions and
madness of crowds. Is thrust into a saddle
and the horse he is impaled on, is impelled
forward leaving the hanging man behind.

Sometimes he is a black man and his
body is defiled.

Another, if he is lucky, the man with
no name will give his victim a rickety perch
to stand on and a bag of gold to retrieve if
he survives. That is, if the man with no
name's aim remains true, as it always has,
from a safe distance, a head start away.

Or, in yet another iteration, a man
and his mistress entertain a black sun idea,
sign a blood oath, a murder suicide? or
double suicide pact, officials can never
really decide which, as the man of letters
left no note behind.

They left matching head wounds,
blood puddles and little else that could be
used as evidence of intent. What seems
clear was that he wanted to try death out to
see how it felt.

Post Card from Meeks, Date Unknown,
Post Marked Oslo: *The Scream*

Must have been still working at the
bar as the image of myself I see, is leaning
out the backdoor of the pub, letting a long,
primal one go. I was stuck in one of those
existential nightmare plays that Sartre
would have written if he'd worked in a bar:
locked in with two, officially-designated-as-
such, bar drunks, listening to their
competing versions of the twilit twisted
place they were currently existing in, and no
way out.

These non-stop talkers, only pausing
to light cigarettes or to hit the head. No
doubt talking to themselves when there was
no one else to listen.

The one working on becoming a
living, landlocked version of Jonah's whale,
was a committed, but transparent liar of the
worst sort. His alternate realities included
stints as a Troy cop, a registered male nurse,
a Vietnam vet, an improbably overweight
called up-because-of-his-expertise army
reservist, a day trader, and so on. I took
mental notes for a while but after each one
was disproved by what he said, I gave up
caring. All you wanted was equal time to
ask a pertinent question, like, "If you are a
registered nurse, why aren't you working as
one?"

The dapper one was an absentee boss's son on an endless lunch break that began as soon as the barman showed up for work and ended some eight or so hours later. If he had contested his divorce, I would have volunteered as a witness for his wife, as I had spent more of his conscious time with him, over the last five or ten years, than she had. Not that all this time spent swilling Bud and burning Merits prevented him from telling everyone who would listen, how hard he was working. Or how many DWI's he had, necessitating multiple name changes on his license. The worst thing, for him, before his stroke, was Motor Vehicles computerizing their files.

A few hours of this, four or five times a week, and you'd be taking scream breaks as well. They didn't help.

Promotional Post Card March 23, 20—
for *Creation Story,* by Steven Owen Shields

An inverted pyramid
contains all the blue
sky and cumulus clouds
left over from first days
of the firmament, settling,
now, high above Earth's
amorphous mass.
Manned flights have not
been invented yet but
a severed hand, gripping
a device that could be
a cell phone or an electronic
device, has slipped through
a hole in time.
The pyramid hovers like
an alien craft from worlds
well-beyond this still-forming
one. What lies below, could
be an ocean or a land mass,
that has not solidified yet.
There could be a story here
but I don't know what it is.

Post Card to Thompson March 26, 20--:
Paris Nocturne

Even the barbarians at the gate,
cannot bear to see Paris burning. The
eternal city lives in our minds, in our
collective memory, even if we have never
been there.

The poet drinks Kronenbourg,
consults visuals, post cards, that show what
the city looks like after dark.

A photo essay, from the thirties,
suggests the Parisian night is for indulging
the flesh. What is most unseemly in the day
time, is normal, once natural light is
withdrawn. Dark artists find comfort, a
second home, in this world among people
who have no morals, whose women offer
their bodies for a reasonable price.

Bright, artificial lights create a
different kind of illusion. Suggest gaiety
that verges on hysteria and seems forced
even in the best of times.

The poet writes his impressions in a
journal, carefully inscribing one thought
after another, creating order where none had
been known to exist.

In the morning he reviews his work
from previous nights. Paris was yesterday.

Post Card to Thompson April 6, 20--:
Naked Lunch

Reading a random page of *Naked Lunch* is enough to transform any man into a beast. What was once a human being reading, is now the torso of a man with a dog's head, a kind of monster wearing a soiled university sweatshirt. Is just another suspecting victim of Dr. Benway's prescriptive language whose words contain messages that extend well beyond the page, words that are absorbed directly through the skin.

The movie being made of this text is how dystopia will look on national TV once drug taking has been made mandatory. Once mainlining false information and completely meaningless images replace free thinking. The artist/author is the one who controls what is released into the air waves. No one escapes the messaging. Anyone who does not recognize this dynamic will become part of the problem and will be eliminated. This is what today looks like tomorrow.

Post Card to Church October 2013

Hey Churchman,

     Last year, day after we left,
Super Storm Sandy (that's what they
called the kickass, no-longer-quite a
hurricane these days) picked up the
Old Harbor dock and deposited it on
land. Washed out the Corn Neck Road,
the dunes, even dropped the stone memorial
to Adrian Block into the surf. Not quite
as bad as the Hurricane of '38 where Block
Island was reported on radio as, "no longer
there", but bad enough. '38 was the year
much of Providence ended up under ten
feet of water and a tidal wave swept over
Long Island, across the Sound and pounded
the Connecticut shore and no one saw it
coming. At least, these days, we have
advance warnings, though hundreds of
thousands ignored them after the previous
year's coastal storm went inland instead,
left the big cities unscathed but devastated
upstate, Western Mass., and Vermont.
We name all the storms now so we have
something to remember them by. We had no
advance warning you were leaving us
forever, man, but we still remember your
name.

Post Card to Thompson April 24, 20--:
Delphine de Vigan's *Nothing Holds Back
the Night*

      Nothing holds back the night.
Not even the novels that could be
memoirs if all the facts were aligned
as if they hadn't taken place. As if the
author's mother had not seized control
of the metro train system and changed
the trajectories of all the lines, describing
arcs at the place where parallel lines meet.
      Everything is true. Even the
narratives that are completely made up.
Even the meta-fictional metaphors where all
the interview tapes used to frame them are
stolen from another person's archival
history. Having extra sensory perception
eases the tension of moving seamlessly
from one world to another.
      So, mother says.
      What mother says is law in that
place where time ends and new world
orders are given.

Post Card to Thompson April 28, 20--:
Girl Dreaming in Blue

"The words of the prophets are written
on the subway walls-tenement halls..."
                    Paul Simon

        Some kind of spilt screen dream
sequence in blue. Of a young woman in
Streetwise, pits of Seattle, street drama.
The woman caught in reverie: part the poem
of someone's disassembling life painted on
concrete wall, part overlay of an: as-seen-
from-a speeding-car window, blur of trees
and clouds dissipating like that drug
induced poem, describing how skin melts
the sky, and the rush of blood that follows,
feels like death on a sunny afternoon.
        All of it like the memory of taking
one of those profiling tests they give to
desperately repressed/distressed youths. A
test designed to reveal interior wounds that
refuse to heal but often uncover something
else: what lies within dreaming that deepens
the crevasse separating us from a world of
pain.
        The first time I took such a test,
I felt the way the depicted young woman
felt: both apart from the world and in other
worlds beyond clear definition; only the
torments overlapping.
        The person in my test picture was a

young man instead of a woman. I was
supposed to make up a story of how he felt,
what he saw, what he was thinking, what he
might do next...

I made up stuff that had no bearing
on any kind of reality in my worlds. I
mused the way the young woman mused,
echoing the sounds of silence.

Post Card to Thompson May 3, 20--

The swan represents the poet's one
time friend's home nearby a pub called
The White Swan where repast may be had.
A meal might include fruits as exotic as a
tangerine or as common as an apple
accompanied by strong ale or beer (not
shown).
If they wrote in tandem, their
notebooks would be open to pages the way
this one is, though stained with by ink blots,
smears where moisture fouls what has been
written down.
Perhaps Coleridge would inscribe
lines from "A Lover's Complaint to His
Mistress" or a "Dream Too Late", while
Wordsworth might be musing on trips
abroad after fording the Thames on
"Waterloo Bridge". The poem on the page
(shown) is too indistinct to read.
Richard Holmes writes in his
biographical notes of STC's opiate abuse,
though the drug of choice would not have
been taken in tablet form, or been dispensed
from a plastic prescription bottle with safety
top removed, as shown here.
The dark avian presence opposite
the swan is a bird of prey that represents
death. There are no daffodils anywhere.

Post Card to Thompson May 6, 20--:
The Poet at Kurt Cobain
Landing wearing a rubber dog mask and
hand painted answers to Kurt C questions,
Private Keep Out

        Cobain wrote an "Anthems for
the Doomed Youth": like the one by
Wilfred Owen but different.
        He'd be a one name rock star if he
were living now. So famous he didn't need
a first and a last one, just a brand name. For
personal appearances all he world have to
do is show, act cool, preen. Just being was
enough.
        Mega.
        Man.
        Went directly from his mansion to
rock and roll heaven with a shot gun in his
mouth.
        Fuck Go, fuck the two hundred
dollars, fuck Courtney Love.
        He was already in Nirvana. What
more could he possibly need?

"I say shot gun, shoot em 'fore he run
now...."
                              Junior Walker

Post Card to Church

Hey Churchman,

Saw an article in the paper just before
we left for Block I would have sent you.
Seems two clowns stole a safe from a
nightclub after a sold-out special
performance with 35 large locked inside.
They emptied the sucker downstate
and dumped it in the Hudson, then called a
cab for Newark, figuring they were good to
go; fifty miles from the gig, empty safe in
the Hudson, unmarked cash in hand, you
had to figure they were in a happy place.
You also had to figure once they got to
Newark, they could hop some overseas
flight and flash the cash until they were
broke and like, who would ever know?
Well, if it sounds too good to be true, it was.
Who knows how John Law figured out
where they were headed and how they were
getting there, but one guess who was
waiting for the suckers when they arrived.
End of story, right? Wrong. We both know
that cabbie didn't get paid. That he was out
tolls, gas and pay. Plus, he would have to
testify. The little man is screwed again, my
friend.

Post Card to Thompson May 4, 20--:
White on White with phrase Puerto Rico
Is Dying

It is not the White Album cover
but the feeling of it. Negation. Becoming
one with the number nine in a black hash
dream, a dream slightly dulled by neat
Seagram's 7 poured on ice. Everything
was poured on ice that year. And the ones
that came after.
This was a year that was destined
not to end well and I remembered the last
time I saw Puerto Rico. How it felt the same
way, minus the ice. How it was worse than
any hash fueled nightmare. Any Bardo
death dream with a thousand demons in it.
How flying into Puerto Rico from
the Virgins I listened as the screaming
woman in the rear of the plane raved. How
she was consumed by hysterical rage
threatening to jump if they would just let
her go. How they didn't and some people
on board wished they would just let her go.
In Ponce they sedated her. Strapped
her down on a flight from Puerto Rico to
NY where the rages got worse. I couldn't
see the water and the green spot of the
island any longer, but I remembered how it
looked, with that woman raving, as we
came to land. How, mornings, on the NY
island, she broke windows with her fists,

first thing, to wake us up. We would never
be more awake than we were then.

After two asylum years, years of
new sedation drugs, ECT, and relapsing into
states of confusion more profound than the
ones she had known before,
she began a project of remapping the world
that had nothing in it you could see from a
plane but New York and what lay beneath.

She would write, "Puerto Rico is
dying," on the foil from Kool cigarette
packets where she kept all her personal
journals.

Hundreds of notes, mostly
impossible to read. She must have wept a
lot describing her Brave No World with no
creatures in it.

Said the first shock treatments made
your brain boil, made your thoughts go
from black and white in color to an awful
white. "Totally fucking white," she said,
"White on white."

Post Card to Thompson, May 10, 20--:
Karen Black, still from *Five Easy Pieces*

     Karen, you look like the day after
the night before. After casting a fistful
of dice against a concrete wall, risking
it all, whispering, "Dem bones, dem bones,
dem pearly bones...." as you rolled, losing
once again...became just another one of a
thousand corpses in a script you wrote,
listening to Patti Smith sing, "Night of a
Thousand Dancers."
     "Do you know how to pony?"
     Surely you did. On acid for real
in New Orleans graveyard up against
a sagging tombstone in *Easy Rider*,
seeing things, no man, or woman, was
meant to see.
     Are you still stripping for Jesus?
     Or have you become just another
surrogate mother for a bad, mad and
dangerous to know gone poet? Conceiving
Ada, Lady Byron's love child, in a twisted,
real, dream with Rob Zombie in the starring
role?
     Did you take turns drinking blood
and wine from a skull with the Angel of
Death? Envisioning that the man in a black
robe, you were consorting with was Tom
Waits, but when you asked the piano man to
play, and croon us a tune, he developed

wings and disappeared, with a covey of
bats, never to be seen again.

What could be worse than that?

Waking up like the girl you no
longer were, not play acting, twenty
minutes late for a twelve-hour shift waiting
greasy spoon tables, uniform still stained by
yesterday's soup of the day.

Not even a piano man can make that
right. Can change the tune, prevent what is
going to happen next.

Post Card to Dickey, Father of Bronwyn,
Kevin and Christopher, Over the White Sea,
June 2, 20--

He flew over the White Sea, a
canteen of "good bourbon and GI Juice" at
his side, sighting the terraced hills, the rice
paper dwellings, the conical hat wearing
farmers bent to the task. A payload of 300
lb. bombs in the hold: gasoline and napalm
ready to be released. Not so much a
deliverance as an annihilation, tsunami of
fire about to be released, destruction far
worse, in terms of lives lost than the atomic
bombs that soon followed.
The whole motion of the rocking
plane something no one could forget, never
knowing how many he killed, how many
died at his command. Not even a hundred
poems, a thousand prayers of forgiveness,
can erase the facts. Even decades later, his
dreams explode in Code Red colors.

Post Card to Church

Hey Churchman.

Been awhile since I've written, I know. Almost a year. What do you say to a dead guy, anyway? Weird thing is, the other day, I was waiting to cross the street downtown and there's this guy parked in a cab, the driver, idling by Proctor's waving at me. Like he knows me, you know? And he's got this long blonde hair and a moustache. Man, I had to look twice.

Kind of freaked me out at first. So, when I got across the street, I had to check the dude out.

Asked, "Do, I like, actually, know you?"

And, he said, "Man, I thought you were this drummer in a band."

I forget the name of the band. Doesn't matter anyway. A drummer, man, it's come to this! I know I can give off a weird vibe but that is the weirdest, most fucked up vibe there is. We used to try and guess which guy was the drummer, at the club, when the new bands were setting up. You can always tell: subtract a couple of chromosomes, scramble some brains, and you have the drummer. Only was wrong once on a couple of years of guessing.

Anyway, I felt since the hack had freaked me out so bad, I'd return the favor. Told him I had this friend who more than kind of looked like him: longhair and shit and he drove a cab too. But, it couldn't have been him 'cause he was dead. Died in his ride, man, tragic.

"Yeah, man, "he said, "That really sucks. See you."

Pulled away like pronto, burning oil as he went just like one of your rides. Fucker didn't even offer to give me a lift.

Post Card to Thompson, June 13, 20-:
Patricia Neal Still from *Hud*

        All the cruel men in her life
have left their marks on her skin.
She has the look of someone who was
never loved but often lusted after. Was
always fleeing as far away from home as
she could, in her dreams, but never quite
making it out of town. Never making it
past a thirty-minute layover bus stop on
the edge of a nowhere place in Texas,
that is post marked as Clyde.
        All this futile fleeing totally
defeats a woman. Leaves her dried out,
like a corn husk with no kernels left
inside.
        All the horsemen in her life pass her
by, without looking, where she stands,
in the dust, holding a suitcase that is
destined for Lost and Found, Unclaimed
Luggage, once it has been loaded in the
hold and she does not board after it.
        Walking home she feels as if her life
was totally unclaimed as well. That her
punched ticket has expired too.

Post Card to Thompson June 26, 20-:
Cancelled Mexican Visa for Frederic Tuten

There you were. In the room where
the white asparagus grew until they touched
the ceiling. Grew through thatched straw
mattress, poking holes in the soot covered,
rag sheets. The artist's corn cob pipe still
warm on the painter's chair. His easel
propped against paint spattered walls,
stretched canvas blood spattered, and
skinned potato smeared.
Vincent's Bad Café closed now.
Packed for moving plank by plank, stone by
stone, to Oaxaca where the British Counsel
drinks Mescal, debating metaphysics with
the worm trapped at the bottom of the
bottle. The air is heavy with volcano dust
and smoke of a thousand torches lit for a
processional on a day for the dead.
The Counsel asks a lady in black,
dealing tarot cards in a dark corner of the
bar, to tell his future by the cards. She says,
"You have no future. Your future's all used
up."
Even the worm agrees.

Post Card to Thompson, June 29, 20-:
Pre-revolutionary Che G. with fiancée

He could be anyone: this dapper
young man with raven hair beauty, plainly,
even conservatively, dressed in button down
long sleeve shirt, slacks and shoes, sitting
on ground for a picnic? Rendezvous? On
campus?
Before the *Motorcycle Diaries*,
journeys into the interior/unknown. Before
the poster boy iconography, the Viva la
Revolucion beret and beard. Before Castro
and other eminent emissaries for the good
fight that can never be won. Before the
fatal shoot out, proof-of- death photos in
South American jungle. Before he became
just another media image for public display,
presaging those equally as unreal
propaganda images of Saddam's dead
psycho sons: Qusay and Uday.
Long before the fame and the
pyrrhic brush with glory, he could be
anyone in a picture with a girl he would
disappoint in love, the girl he would never
marry.

Post Card to Thompson July 03, 20-:
Iseult Gonne When Young

     "Iseult is mad aygan," Maud would
have written to Yeats if she were a poet
instead of a revolutionary. Though what she
said, was, her daughter, then a teen, was
mad.
     Willful is what she meant.
     Her mother's daughter.
     Yeats expressed sympathy.
     Proposed: to the mother and the
daughter. Having failed to woo his soul
mate, the Queen of Ireland, Maud Gonne,
he tried the daughter. Who he had known
since she was a child. Who he was a kind of
surrogate father for? Was even rumored to
Be the father of.
     And was refused.
     Accounts differ on how seriously
she viewed the proposal. Yeats, no doubt,
viewed her rejection as a scornful, Hamlet
rebuke à: from a Hyperion to a satyr.
     The rejection of the famed poet/
playwright probably the most sensible thing
she ever did.
     Allowed Yeats to marry Georgie,
the "automatic writer", who would have a
major role in his life's work as muse,
amanuensis and second tier soul mate.
     Instead, Iseult, married a younger,
feckless, "imbecile", according to Yeats.
One who would become a second-rate
novelist, probably totally forgotten now, if

61

he hadn't become a traitor; an Irish Pound, broadcasting Nazi propaganda for the Germans during the war.

What must have Iseult thought as a single mother, deserted, at home with two children, no income? Of her strange metempsychosis life: from a young woman, a future Nobel Laureate's wrote poems about, to a lonely, harried mom, the kind of woman who harbored a German parachutist/fugitive; a man she confessed to loving and somehow, still managing to beat the rap, to be acquitted at the subsequent trial. No: Berlin Mon Amour, movie made of her life and times.

All of it so weirdly Wagnerian now. A kind of opera with no heroes, no musical score, no lovers left alive.

Post Card to Thompson July 18, 20-:
Excerpt from Siegfried Sassoon
poem with young man in idyllic
setting reading verse

Sorrows of Young Siegfried.
The only fields he may have seen in
his youth may would have had the name
Flanders on them. Had trenches filled with
mud, the bodies of his soldiers, and a view
of barbed wire, a no man's land without
end.
Dawn Breaking with Mustard Gas
could have been the name of one of his war
poems but wasn't.
"Trench Duty" was.

"Blank stare. I'm wide awake,
and some chap's dead."

All the Sorrows of Young Siegfried,
real.

Post Card to Thompson August 13, 20-:
Nelson Algren walking on the streets of Chi
Town

Dreaming of Simone, of Chicago's
own Monarch Beer, neon wilderness Liquor
sign, blur of street car, beat down, fare
game, red lights hustlers, slumlord pay by
day flophouse rooms, candle lit and
cigarette smoked, bedside table,
overflowing ash heap, peeled label, long
necked brown bottle empties; Dago red,
vino stained, chipped glass containers,
tipped high hat johnnie red, amber colored
pints; Darktown, saloon nights and rumpled
sheet days, jazzed police reefer raids,
speakeasy johns and sharp duds pimps; man
with a horn, man with a golden arm, man
walking the wild side, loaded dice
game defeated, beating a portable royal to
death; novel ends and no new beginnings,
doomed-to-fail transatlantic affair, oceans of
morbidity and grief, his love token, hers, to
the grave.

Post Card to Thompson August 27, 20-:
Jeanne Moreau Noire

        The bar she is drinking in
has been leached of all color so that
everything inside is either black or
white. The Kir cocktail on the café
table for two is as dark as the room
she is sitting in and the dead-center-of-
the-table candle has no wax left to melt
the remaining luster from her eyes.
        The door that opens stirs low
hanging clouds of smoke but does not
admit the man she once thought of as
a lover. On a low, spot-lit stage, a past-
her-prime chanteuse promises that when
all else fails there is always love.
        The actress drinks a third Kir as
if she were swallowing all the darkness
she can before the night ends. There is
never enough night where she is living
now and there never would be.

Post Card to Thompson September 14, 20-:
Arthur Miller and Marilyn Monroe in NYC

Miller didn't marry her for
her mind. Nor did any of the others
who went with her. A fact that must
have weighed on her as she began to see
herself as no longer young. The future,
especially for a woman, one who depended
on her looks for self-esteem, is murder.
Had Marilyn, famously
photographed reading *Ulysses,* made it past
the part that said: "Stately, plump, Buck
Mulligan..." without asking a dozen
questions?
Arthur would have said, "He's
outdoors, on the top of a Martello Tower,
where they live. Mulligan is the narrator's
roommate and he's looking in a mirror,
preparing for a morning shave..." The sun
catches the mirror, a blinding, flashing
light....
And *Ulysses* becomes more
confusing after that. A whole lot more.
Maybe not as bad as *Sound and the Fury,*
but damn close. She hadn't made it past
page two on that one.
There was no story, no plot, who
were the characters....it was all just words
on a page.
After the photo, you can imagine her
removing those, made-her-look intelligent
reading glasses. She'll look towards the
photographer. Then toward her husband.

She's beautiful. Absolutely gorgeous.

Somewhere a radio is playing, "All of me, why not take all of me..."

Post Card to Thompson: Sept 16, 20-:
Young woman in white descending a
staircase

    If you worked the graveyard, in
a bar long enough, she's going to show up.
    You never know what she's going
to look like or how she'll be dressed.
She might have a look like Dale Evans,
or a NASCAR honey. Might look like
a hippie chick lost in time or Marlene
after her last night shift at the Blue Angel...
    She'll order a classic cocktail.
One only the veterans know how to make.
Maybe a sidecar, a stinger...
    She likes them chilled to-the-bone-
cold, served up, and how it feels, how it
burns going down.
    She'll order one for a guy down
the bar. That guy who never talks to anyone.
The one who pretends to watch the game
but is watching something only he can see.
    She'll move in nice and close and
say, "Go on, try it. Take a sip. They're nice
and sweet."
    And he will. They always do. The
temptation is too great not to.
    When they find him, the discovery
might make the paper. Just as often it
doesn't. Who was he, really? Just another
nobody who satin bars. He was there and
then he wasn't.
    Who cares?
    I do.

Last Post Card from Steve D:
Original Collage June 20-

The background feels Futuristic.
Feels otherworldly like a PK Dick
phantasm. A Minority Report just before the
pre-crime unit descends in force.
Blackbirds peck at the head of a
woman whose wig is on fire. A Difference
Engine implanted in her brain powers the
machines that traverse the space between
her head and the man on the opposite side
of the image.
Twin black adders protrude from his
head just above the place where the ears
would be if they were attached to his head.
A black man is pointing at the tiny
fellow ensconced on a table secured to the
snake bearer's head.
Disembodied, all seeing eyes, killer
drones, crocks of gin, and floating tea cups
float in the weightless sky as if impelled by
a solar wind.
What is on the peripherals will
determine the fate of this tenuous world.
All we can see are the edges of
things: a man falling from a great height, a
portrait of youth from another time, hands
clasped as if in prayer.

Post Card to Thompson Sept. 29, 20-:
A series of Foto Booth pictures
of adult couple with and without shades

      Their wallet sized, four to a strip,
snaps are their audition for a screen test.
Fifteen minutes of fame among the
immortals if selected. More foto marts if
they are not.
      Warhol's gallery lives on even as
the subjects die off. So many ways to die
too young. Tragic deaths all of them. Drugs
mostly. It was the sixties and everyone is
doing something or else expecting rain. the
riskier the behavior, the better.
      The ones who survived are the star-
crossed ones. Are the battered angels on
Desolation Row or down on Highway 51.
      Edie, Nico, Viva, Lou Reed,
things do go better with coke, Bobby D,
The girl with one tear, Valerie Solanas with
a gun. All those Chelsea Girls and boys.
From Sedgwick to Woronov and all the
waking, fallen angels in between.

Post Card to Thompson, October 1, 20-:
Asian woman in a bar with
a drunk man draping arm over
her shoulder, his head turned away

Her expression is somewhere
between terminally bored and how-did-
my-life-end-up-this way. Sitting in some
karaoke club, empty Nippon bottles on
table, half-filled carafe of clear liquid,
maybe booze, maybe not, and a corked
bottle, label unseen, among the clutter.
Her low-cut, black, eveningwear
suggests she is dressed for a high priced
trick. No by-the-hour love motel at the
end of this night, but a suite somewhere
downtown with a sauna, a queen-sized bed,
a roomy place to change in, once the john
passes out.
When it is time to leave, she tucks
the credit card receipt for services rendered,
in her small, only-the-essentials purse, with
the cash tip he forgot to give her, that she
extracted from his wallet, leaving him
enough to tip the bell boy and the maids.
He won't complain about the
missing money.
They never do.

Post Card to Thompson: October 14, 20-:
Beehive hairdo working girl on the job with
a lit cigarette

One of her former occupations,
the one she put on her tax forms, must have
been: Go Go Dancer. Even she has to admit,
it was a job with a limited future but some
side benefits. A few months of this and she
was ready to pursue her side job, outside, on
the street, though with less clothes than she
used as a dancer, more makeup, and no
musical accompaniment.
	If asked about her work, she'd shrug
and reply, "I prefer outdoor work, anyway.
	The only smoke that gets in my eyes
there is my own."
	Not that most of her work was
actually outside. Except for cheap tricks
when business was exceptionally bad. Out
there, smoke wasn't the worst thing she had
to worry about getting in her eyes.

Post Card to Church from Block Island:
Late October 20-

Hey Churchman,

They replaced the bench I used to sit on to write these annual cards to you from the Island. Never thought they would, as it was poured, molded concrete. Maybe the tourists stole them.

There are brightly painted picnic tables on the small, open-air veranda now. Kind of throwback hippie art forms to go with the back-to-nature vegetarian café next to the bookstore.

You'd probably hate the sentiment. Despite your long hair, your neatly groomed beard and moustache, you were a political troglodyte by my liberal standards. I expect you thought most hippies were better off dead. Sometimes I wonder how we got along.

The café is closed now. Just about everything is but the bookstore. Reading books knows no season. Nor does the writing of them. It's what we writers do. Did, in your case.

Writing is as good a reason as any to go on. A way to keep memories alive. People too, I guess. Otherwise, there is no point in remembering anything at all.

Post Card to Thompson Late October 20-:
Marquee advertising Warhol & the Velvet
Underground + Nico

All the Chelsea Girls were nodding
on psychedelic pillows:
Super Star Woronov. Super Star Viva.
International Velvet. Edie ...who remembers
who else? And the boys were there too:
Morrissey, Malanga, Joe D, Andy... None
of them were sure what movie they were in
or what lines they were supposed to say.
Whether what was being filmed was
an amateur porn flick, with professionals, or
high art. As long as no one died it would be
all right. Dying would come later. After the
cameras were turned off.
If there was a script, Andy had it.
Andy always had a script. Somewhere. If
there was one, he would have it. Just ask
and he'd say something vague. He'd even
hand you some papers that might have said
anything. He didn't expect anyone to read
it. No one ever did. Andy could have been
president.
After the inauguration there would
be a wake for fallen angels. It would be the
trippiest, most happening party ever.
Everyone would want to go. But anyone
who was there wouldn't remember a thing
but they would say they did. And make shit
up about what came down. Andy would
have liked that.

Post Card to Costa, Oct. 02, 20-:
Prepaid generic postcard

You sent me dozens of these
over the years when you didn't have
the time or the energy to write real
letters. Mostly to talk baseball. A habit
you picked up from Dave Markson until
you had a falling out over a Yankees/
Red Sox game. 20 years or so of literary
and personal reflections flushed away in
one brief note.
I'm watching you're A's lose in
the wild card game to the Rays thinking
you were the ultimate fan following them
from Shibe Park in Philly to KC and now
out in Oakland.
You suffered with them for 90
years from perennial league doormats to
Charley O's colorful band of misfit
Mavericks; those big time, legendary
winners, until free agency claimed them all.
I wish you were watching them now.
Somehow, they snuck in the bottom of the
playoffs and almost advanced. It was
the kind of long shot you loved. Sometimes
a miracle happens. In horse racing and
baseball but not so much in life.

Post Card to Thompson, Nov. 21, 20-:
Arthur Koestler and his wife relaxing
outdoors

Stalin assured the man
he would experience
Communism up close
and personal.
Had him consigned to
a prison where he could
see, and hear, the daily
executions of his comrades.
Somehow, he was spared
and released, like Dostoevsky
though not nearly as immortal.
Felt that this time in prison
was a prime example of
the God that failed,
the darkness of morning,
noon, and night.
In the end, killing himself
made the most sense of all.
Even his wife thought so too
A suicide pact is forever.

Post Card to Thompson, Nov, 22, 20-:
Hopper, Dennis, Mug Shot, Taos, N.M.

His mug shot is a life
study for one of Lucien
Freud's gallery of human
grotesques. Hopper might
have been out partying with
Jackson or, maybe Bacon in
his Rembrandt abattoir anatomy
phase, looking half dead himself.
You could easily imagine him
traversing the country on a high
handle bars Harley using drug
deal money to buy rocket fuel.
Or see him mortally injured
by the side of some two lane
outside of east jesus, his flaming
bike, nearby, about to explode,
And in the photo shot after
the crash, as a corpse, no
one wanted to identify.

Post Card to RTS in the Otherworld 12/19

I thought about you while half-watching one of those 70's shoot 'em up, Dirty Harry Callahan flicks. Clint chasing some bad guy through the street of San Francisco, big-assed gun ready to make someone's day. It should have been obvious that all of your best lines came from movies. But it wasn't the punch lines that made me think of you, it was the cars...cars like you mom's Satellite you modified with a Toyota. The wildest part being it wasn't your fault, no one was badly injured, and the bat-out-of-hell Toyota kid got run in for driving drunk, without a license, in a rental.

The cops weren't really interested in you, given the totaled Dodge wreck was blocking traffic on the busiest intersections between Albany and Schenectady and what was left of the Toyota at rest on the supper club lawn, that bar I was running.
I always meant to ask; How the fuck Did you pass that Breath Test?

Post Card to Thompson, Dec. 07, 20-:
Portrait of the Not So Young Artist as a Dog

The man/dog sitting at a blond wood bar. A fresh poured Miller High Life, from a can, next to a pile of post card he is writing inscriptions on. Dozens of post cards, dozens of inscriptions. All the same.

It's not a Dylan Thomas kind of bar. Not the White Horse. Or McSorley's. Or any of a hundred low down and dirty NYC watering holes. Not one cigarette burning, no young acolytes clamoring or a recitation, crazy talk, with the bard of Wales. No White Giant's Thigh. No musings on Fern Hill. Just a silent TV, on a far bar wall showing a sporting event of the season. A clean well lit, picture window, place.

Dylan is in that other place. That bar where he is backed up to eternity. Setting the bar record for shots consumed. A record no one would ever break after massive alcohol insult to brain and body. No beer bucket specials where he has gone. No live music. Ever. Just a wife and daughter left behind with leftover life to live.

Both of them gone now too.

Post Card to Church: A Diary of the Plague
Years

I missed writing cards for a couple
of years. I thought of you, though, but no
one was going anywhere for over a year.
Certainly not on a ferry, to an island where
they had enough troubles of their own
without importing any.
Everyone gets to wear a mask
inside now especially on public transport.
They have this new thing called Uber which
almost makes driving a cab obsolete. You
would have hated it though the idea of
being an independent contractor probably
would appeal to you. It's not really
Libertarian though, believe me.
Working in bars is kind of a thing
of the past too. Who would have thought
that was even possible? I know it would
have done it for me. I have enough trouble
dealing with the political assholery on TV
much less in public. And I know eight out
of ten guys at the bar would have been
dead-set against anything sensible and
agreed one hundred and ten per cent with
the mad man who was president.
I can't see you wearing a mask
but I don't see you buying the so-called
president's bullshit either. You had a strong
BS detector. He's gone now, more or less,
but the plague is back. It may never go way.
You don't know what you're missing.
Lucky you.

9 788182 539501